W9-AWG-494

ABOUT THE BANK STREET READY-TO-READ SERIES

More than seventy-five years of educational research, innovative teaching, and quality publishing have earned The Bank Street College of Education its reputation as America's most trusted name in early childhood education.

Because no two children are exactly alike in their development, the Bank Street Ready-to-Read series is written on three levels to accommodate the individual stages of reading readiness of children ages three through eight.

○ *Level 1:* **GETTING READY TO READ (Pre-K–Grade 1)**
Level 1 books are perfect for reading aloud with children who are getting ready to read or just starting to read words or phrases. These books feature large type, repetition, and simple sentences.

● *Level 2:* **READING TOGETHER (Grades 1–3)**
These books have slightly smaller type and longer sentences. They are ideal for children beginning to read by themselves who may need help.

○ *Level 3:* **I CAN READ IT MYSELF (Grades 2–3)**
These stories are just right for children who can read independently. They offer more complex and challenging stories and sentences.

All three levels of The Bank Street Ready-to-Read books make it easy to select the books most appropriate for your child's development and enable him or her to grow with the series step by step. The levels purposely overlap to reinforce skills and further encourage reading.

We feel that making reading fun is the single most important thing anyone can do to help children become good readers. We hope you will become part of Bank Street's long tradition of learning through sharing.

The Bank Street College of Education

For William Robert Davies
— W.H.H.

For Karin
— P.C.

For a free color catalog describing Gareth Stevens' list of high-quality books and multimedia programs, call 1-800-542-2595 (USA) or 1-800-461-9120 (Canada). Gareth Stevens Publishing's Fax: (414) 225-0377.
See our catalog, too, on the World Wide Web: http://gsinc.com

Library of Congress Cataloging-in-Publication Data

Hooks, William H.
   The Gruff brothers / by William H. Hooks; illustrated by Pierre Cornuel.
     p. cm. -- (Bank Street ready-to-read)
   Summary: A retelling, in rebus format, of the traditional tale in which three clever billy goats outwit a big, ugly troll.
   ISBN 0-8368-1749-4 (lib. bdg.)
   1. Rebuses. [1. Fairy tales. 2. Folklore--Norway. 3. Rebuses.] I. Cornuel, Pierre, ill. II. Title. III. Series.
PZ8.H77Gr 1997
398.2'09481'04529648
[E]--DC21   97-1366

This edition first published in 1997 by
Gareth Stevens Publishing
1555 North RiverCenter Drive, Suite 201
Milwaukee, Wisconsin 53212 USA

Printed in Mexico

1 2 3 4 5 6 7 8 9 01 00 99 98 97

Bank Street Ready-to-Read™

The Gruff Brothers

by William H. Hooks
Illustrated by Pierre Cornuel

A Byron Preiss Book

Gareth Stevens Publishing
MILWAUKEE

There once was a meadow
full of animals. There was . . .

a red fox,

a green snake,

a white sheep,

a yellow duck,

a blue bird,

4

and **3** billy goats.

They were brothers,

and their last name was Gruff.

The animals called the  billy goat Little Gruff because he was the smallest.

They called the **black** billy goat Middle Gruff
because he was bigger than Little Gruff.

They called the **black** and /white/

billy goat Fiddle Gruff

because he played the fiddle.

He was the biggest of the brothers

and had long pointy horns.

The brothers spent their days
eating sweet green  grass
and tasty yellow flowers.

But at night, big Fiddle Gruff
would play his fiddle,
and all the animals would dance.

The  fox and snake

made a funny couple.

The bird flapped her wings.

The  sheep and duck

whirled around

and around.

Little Gruff and

Middle Gruff tap-danced

while Fiddle Gruff played.

Their 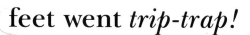 feet went *trip-trap!*

Trip-trap! Trip-trap!

But before too long,

all the sweet green  grass

and the tasty yellow flowers

were eaten up.

The animals were soon too hungry
and too tired to dance.

One day Little Gruff said,

"Look at that  bridge.

I see sweet green grass

and tasty yellow flowers

on the other side of the river.

Let's go over the bridge!"

"I wouldn't!"

shouted the red 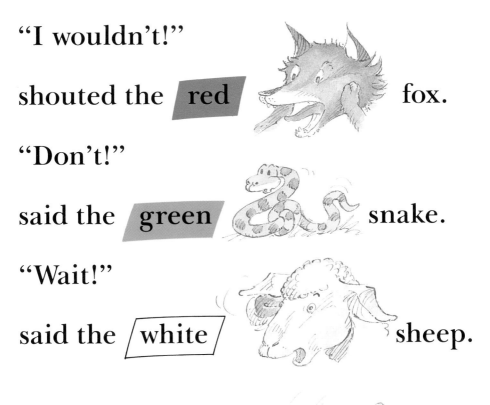 fox.

"Don't!"

said the green snake.

"Wait!"

said the /white/ sheep.

"Hold on!"

said the yellow  duck.

"You can't do that!"

said the blue bird.

13

"Why not?" asked Little Gruff.

"Because," said Middle Gruff.

"Because why?" asked Little Gruff.

"Because a wicked troll guards

the bridge," said Fiddle Gruff.

"What's a troll?" asked Little Gruff.

"I'll tell you," said his big brother.

"He has 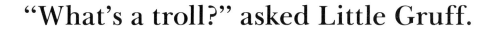 eyes as big as saucers.

He has a  nose as long

and crooked as a  snake.

He has  teeth

like a tiger's,

and green shaggy hair."

All of the animals were afraid

of the troll.

But Little Gruff said, "I am going

over the  bridge."

Trip-trap! Trip-trap!

He started over.

The troll roared,

Who's that trip-trapping over my bridge?

"It's only me, Little Gruff.

I'm going over the  bridge

to eat green grass."

17

> I'm going to gobble you up!

roaded the ![troll] troll.

"Oh, no! Don't eat me,"
said Little Gruff.
"I'm much too small.
Wait until Middle Gruff crosses.
He's much bigger than I am."
"Oh, pickles and popcorn,"
said the troll.

"You are much too small.
Go on over the bridge."

So Little Gruff went across—
trip-trap, trip-trap—
and into the meadow.
There he began to eat
sweet green grass
and tasty yellow flowers.

"I can fool that  troll, too,"
said Middle Gruff.
Trip-trap! Trip-trap!
He started over the bridge.
The troll roared,

Who's that
trip-trapping over
my bridge?

"It's only me, Middle Gruff.
And I am looking
for sweet green  grass."

I am going to
gobble you up!

"Don't do that," said Middle Gruff.
"I'm too small.

Wait until Fiddle Gruff crosses.
He's much bigger than I am."
"Oh, pickles and popcorn!"
roared the troll.

"I am very, very hungry.
And you are too small.
Go on across."

Soon, great big Fiddle Gruff saw
his brothers eating
sweet green  grass
on the other side
of the bridge.

Trip-trap! Trip-trap!
He raced onto the bridge.

The  troll roared,
"Who's that trip-trapping
over my bridge?"
"It's me, Fiddle Gruff,
and I'm very, very hungry."
"Me, too," roared the troll.
"I'm going to gobble you up."

AND HERE
I COME!

The troll's  eyes as big

as  saucers were popping.

His  nose as long

as a crooked  snake

was twitching.

His 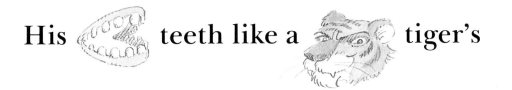 teeth like a tiger's

were grinding as he roared.

Big Fiddle Gruff was afraid.

He wanted to run.

But he didn't turn back.

Instead, he lowered his

long pointy horns.

And he butted the  troll

with all his might.

The troll flew off the bridge

and tumbled back into the river.

The last anyone saw of him, he was swimming away as fast as his shaggy green arms could paddle.

Then . . .

the red 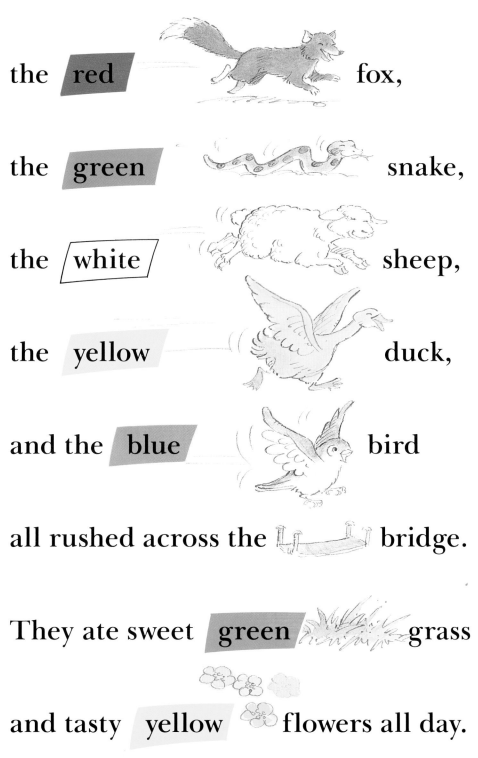 fox,

the green snake,

the white sheep,

the yellow duck,

and the blue bird

all rushed across the bridge.

They ate sweet green grass

and tasty yellow flowers all day.

29

That night, when the  stars
came out
and the moon
was bright,
Fiddle Gruff played his fiddle
while . . . the fox,

the  snake, the sheep,
the duck, and the bird
flapped and clapped.
And Middle Gruff and Little Gruff
tap-danced.
Trip-trap! Trip-trap! Trip-trap!

William H. Hooks is the author of many books for children, including the highly acclaimed *Moss Gown*. He is also the Director of Publications at Bank Street College. As part of Bank Street's Media Group, he has been closely involved with such projects as the well-known Bank Street Readers and Discoveries: An Individualized Reading Program. Mr. Hooks lives with three cats in a Greenwich Village brownstone in New York City.

Pierre Cornuel attended the Ecole Superieure d'Arts Modernes and currently resides in Paris, France. He has illustrated more than 20 books for children since 1980 and was a featured illustrator at the Bologna Book Fair in 1987 and 1988. This is Mr. Cornuel's first book for an American audience.